I0465154

MAKE IT REAL

How to stop thinking and start building

Chris Turner

ISBN: 1523699183
ISBN-13: 978-1523699186

I dedicate this book to my son, Logan, whose sense of wonder inspires me to see the world with fresh eyes.

CONTENTS

ACKNOWLEDGMENTS

This book would not have been possible without the outstanding contributions of some of my favorite people.

- - - - - - - - - - - - - - - - - -

To my wife Hannah, you inspire everyone you meet to be themselves. You are my blue whale, and I'm your giant squid. I love you, sweetheart.

To my business partner Justin Richards, you are the ultimate swiss army knife. This book is testimony to your patience, hard work, and enduring faith in God.

To my parents, you made my life possible. When I fell, you were there to pick me up. When I argued, you listened patiently. Thank you so much for being exactly who you are.

To my sister Carolyn, thanks for always being goofy with me. Our childhood was full of laughs and great stories, and there's no one in the world I'd rather share those memories with.

To Lior Weinstein, Kevin Sandlin, The Iron Yard, Switchyards, and Atlanta Tech Village, thank you for making a difference in the journey of Tenrocket and that of countless entrepreneurs.

To anyone who trusted Tenrocket with taking their idea and making it real, thank you so much for your faith in us. This book would not be possible without you.

INTRODUCTION

It's January 4, 2016, and I have no idea what to name this book. What I do know is that I'm tired of starting each new year with the goal of writing a book, only to see the ball drop 364 days later with nothing published. As I write this introduction, I'm struck by the parallels of writing a book and launching a startup. Much of this book will cover the latter, but I find it interesting how both goals frequently wind up in one's list of New Years Resolutions. Having now checked off the 'start a company' box, I apply the insights and truths learned over the past two years in this book. I remember the feeling of crippling uncertainty and fear before starting Tenrocket, and even though I've now conquered those fears to some degree, my hands are shaking as I finish this sentence. Perhaps this feeling is a necessary barrier to any endeavor worthy of pursuit.

Back in October 2013, I was working on a web application I genuinely believed would revolutionize the education sector. As a professional fundraiser for a nonprofit organization known for teaching entrepreneurship to K-12 students, I had myself convinced that I knew what to do. During nights, weekends, and spare time at work, I hammered away at pitch decks, wireframes, logos, company names, and elaborate business plans. Everything looked great on the outside. It sure had the appearance of a startup. The problem - unbeknownst to me - was that I was building a big, beautiful shell around an extremely tiny, almost invisible hermit crab. As I worked on everything 'external' that people could see, I was neglecting the 'meat' of my app that made it functional. My efforts came to a head in January 2015 when I started calling developers.

Not knowing a thing about code, I called every freelancer and agency in town to get a quote for my app. It didn't take long to discover a fundamental barrier to entrepreneurship: apps are expensive. The cheapest quote I ever received from an agency was $25,000. Most quotes came in the $50k range, and I even received one quote for $250,000. As a nonprofit fundraiser, even the cheapest quote was approaching my annual salary at the time. To make matters worse, my wife had just quit her job to move with me to Atlanta.

With agencies out of the question, I turned my attention to freelancers. As with most new entrepreneurs, my first thought immediately went to finding someone to build my app for equity. It didn't take long to discover that most good developers are far too busy to take on equity projects full time. That left me with one option: paying a freelancer. In my search, I found quite a few great developers willing to build my app for less than $25k. The problem was more with me. As a non-technical founder, I had no idea what to do or say to prevent myself from being ripped off. I heard countless nightmare stories from entrepreneurs who started an app with a freelancer, only to have that project drag on for months and cost thousands of dollars more than initial projections. One founder in particular worked with a developer for six months and paid $50,000, only to receive an app that was little more than fancy wireframes at the end.

Uncomfortable going it alone with freelancers, and unable to pay an agency tens of thousands of dollars, I decided to learn how to code myself. I enrolled in a 3-month coding accelerator in Atlanta called The Iron Yard, and ultimately gained enough experience with Ruby on Rails to be considered a Junior Developer. As part of my final project, I built a minimum viable product (more on that later) for my education app in 10 business days. What struck me most was that I was able to build a functional application in ten days as a Junior Developer with only three months of experience.

"Just *imagine* what Senior Developers can do.", I thought. With that, the idea for Tenrocket was born.

While my company builds web and mobile applications in ten business days for $10k, that's not the purpose of this book. This book is about the lessons learned along the way, including those learned from the startups we've helped launch. The past year and a half have graced me with tremendous insight into what makes a successful startup founder, and this book is the result of that insight.

Top five things you should know about this book:

1. **It's not polished.** I'm writing it in ten business days and giving myself ten additional business days of Quality Assurance before publishing. That leaves little room for fancy illustrations, interviews from experts, and other things you might have grown to expect from startup books.

2. **But that's kind of the point.** By writing a book in ten business days, I set out to prove that you can accomplish hard things (like launching a startup) much faster than you might imagine.

3. **It's not black and white.** The insights I share may or may not apply to you and your idea. We're all unique individuals with our own ideas, and that leaves a lot of room for gray areas. I encourage you to actively question what you read and share any thoughts or criticism with me at chris@tenrocket.com

4. **This book is about going from idea to startup.** Most books, articles, and blog posts about entrepreneurship are *actually* about building and growing a startup or company.

5. **Entrepreneurs frequently struggle with depression and anxiety.** I want you to know you can always reach out to me if you're feeling down. Even though I may not know you, I care a lot about you.

MINDSET

The Real Gap

Take a minute to think about your life. If you're like most people, you've made some mistakes, miscalculations, and errors in judgement along the way. At times you may have held strong opinions and assumptions about the world, only to have them shattered by experience and new insights you were previously blind to.

You look back at those moments and think, "Wow, what was I thinking?". Yet here you are, reading this book in an effort to learn something new and take a positive step forward in your life. What an amazing journey.

Now consider something for a moment - what if you were never born? What if a higher presence reversed your existence, making your failures, successes, relationships, and memories disappear?

Kind of depressing, right? It's sad to consider any life - even a tragic one - suddenly removed from existence. In the startup universe, we tend to look at existing companies and weigh their value based on observable successes and failures.

What most people miss are the companies that never see the light of day. These companies will never know the beauty of improving the life of a person in need because they stay trapped in the minds of their creators.

They will never hire that amazing new college grad who will go on to become a future VP, nor will they will empower their creator to move beyond the corporate grind and feel the incredible power of bringing an idea to life. These companies never even become startups. Instead, they're trapped in the cage of the human mind. I call this *The Real Gap*, and it's the leading cause of death in the startup universe.

The majority of startups don't die from lack of funding, bad product, or weak leadership. They die because they never move past the idea stage. For the sake of clarity, let's define a few terms.

Idea: a suggestion as to a possible course of action.
Startup: a newly established business.
Company: a commercial business.

Here's the funny thing about startups - from the beginning of their life, they're almost *predestined* to die. In fact if you Google the statistics on startup success, you'll find that most startups - **90% of them** - fail to make it past the first year.

Most people look at that statistic and think "Wow, startups are risky!", but we have yet to document the same statistics for *idea* failure. Consider for a moment that 51 percent of working-age US citizens believe there are good opportunities for starting businesses. That sounds great until you realize that only 14 percent - 27 million people - are starting or running new businesses. That's a difference of 37% of the population, or **71 million** people.

Let's say all 71 million of those people crossed *The Real Gap* and turned their ideas into startups. We know already that 90% of those startups - 63.9 million - will fail. That seems shocking at first until you realize that the amount left over - 7.1 million startups - will succeed.

You may be thinking, "Still, that's *a lot* of failed startups", and you'd be right. But the numbers actually favor the successes. Let's assume the average startup costs $50k to create - an estimate that's likely too high on the aggregate.

If all failed startups produce zero return on investment for their founders, we arrive at a total loss of $3.2 trillion. Sounds ridiculously high, right? Not so fast.

Let's say the average successful startup earns $500,000 over the course of its lifetime, an absurdly small number given that dozens of unicorns (companies with a valuation of at least $1 billion) started in the last five years alone.

Given those conservative estimates, we arrive at a total surplus of $3.55 trillion.

$3.55 trillion surplus - $3.2 trillion loss = $.35 trillion surplus

That's $350 billion!

You may be thinking "Who cares about $350 billion? I have a 90% chance of losing $50k and a 10% chance of gaining $500k." The answer is very straightforward and probably won't surprise you. Your goal is to *reduce* the risk of failure (down from 90%), *lessen* the cost of starting (down from $50k), and *increase* your chance of success (up from 10%).

Your first step is crossing *The Real Gap* by moving from idea to startup. The world is full of awful startups, but the single redeeming fact about those startups is that they *exist* and matter to people. Your goal is to make a startup that exists. While this book focuses on figuring out how to do just that, the advice and tools I share will drastically increase your odds of moving from startup to company down the road.

The Perfection Loop

When a startup founder comes up with a new idea, the temptation is to perfect and polish. I know this firsthand having worked on my education app before learning how to code. Rather than focusing on pre-sales, talking to potential users, and getting a very minimal working prototype off the ground, I was designing pitch decks, calling expensive agencies, and looking for investors. I even wrote our brand personality, which is a comically ironic thing to do at the idea stage. If you don't have sales and find yourself working on any of these things, you're stuck in what I call *The Perfection Loop*. It looks something like this:

NEW IDEA

REFINE   STRATEGIZE

SEEK INVESTMENT

Say your friend Kyle has a new idea he describes as Uber for ice cream. "Ice cream trucks are dead!", says Kyle. "I will revolutionize the ice cream delivery market and put it in the cloud!".

Kyle names his idea Kreemy and convinces himself that this idea is the next Facebook, largely because he Googled 'size of ice cream market' yesterday and found that it's projected to be a $54.7 billion dollar industry this year. "If we can capture just one percent market share in five years, we'll be a $547 million company!"

Not knowing how to code, Kyle gets to work on nights and weekends building everything he can to demonstrate the awesomeness of Kreemy. He starts with a business plan and writes a compelling argument for why Kreemy will be a household name in three years. Kyle builds financial projections, develops a marketing strategy, and even writes out his company values.

With his business plan in place, Kyle takes to his computer and mocks up the wireframes for Kreemy. He's not a designer, but he's able to piece together a nice-looking presentation by mimicking other successful apps. He uses these wireframes and his completed business plan to build out a robust pitch deck in PowerPoint, complete with three impressive looking graphs and a team slide showcasing his prospective first hires.

With everything but the actual app built, Kyle officially changes his LinkedIn title to CEO at Kreemy. Following the advice of an article he read in *Entrepreneur Magazine* back in 2011, he incorporates Kreemy as an LLC.

Kyle now feels ready to speak with investors. The big city agency he called last month quoted him at $50k, so he decides to ask for that amount, in exchange for 10% equity. There's also the option to find a technical co-founder, and Kyle knows a guy who knows an excellent programmer. They're meeting for coffee next Thursday.

Fast forward three months, and Kyle has managed to meet with a few investors. Two of them were dead-ends, but one expressed interest in continuing the conversation. It's been several weeks since that pitch, but for some reason the investor seems to be taking his time responding to Kyle's emails. The programmer he met a few months back would have been a great fit, but was far too busy to take on an equity project.

Convinced that his idea needs refinement, Kyle goes back to the drawing board. He cleans up his pitch deck and moves it from PowerPoint to Prezi. Kyle updates his business plan to give it more *modest* financial projections, which now estimate Kreemy to be a $50 million company in three years, *conservatively*. He Googles "startup events" in his area and decides to place more focus on networking. Kyle also applies for several accelerators around the country, convinced that someone will see the vision for Kreemy. After all, it's far too big of an opportunity to pass on.

If you spend a little time in the startup universe, it won't take long to meet someone like Kyle. In truth, it's entirely possible that you're the Kyle in your network. Take a minute and open your LinkedIn profile. If your title contains the word "entrepreneur" or the name of an idea that doesn't have sales or active users, you're probably stuck in *The Perfection Loop*. Some entrepreneurs get trapped for years. Have you ever met an entrepreneur who has been working on the same idea for more than two years, but has no sales or users? I know a founder at eight years and counting.

If you find yourself stuck in *The Perfect Loop* and want to get out, just make a sale. When another person buys your product, that's the moment you become a real entrepreneur. You may be thinking "How can I sell something that doesn't exist?" More on that later. For now, let's continue building the correct mindset to get you there.

The Consumption Trap

Quick, think of someone famous.
Creator.

There's a reason the most successful people are creators, and it's the same reason so few people in the world aren't ridiculously successful. Creating something original is *incredibly* difficult. Just look at some of the barriers facing creators:

    The world is full of things that already exist.
    It's impossible to create something for free.
    Humans are inclined to seek safety and familiarity.
    Humans don't always act in their best interest.

And the greatest barrier of all? The world is constantly telling us to **consume**.

In 1945, the average adult consumed 5.2 hours of media per day. In 2014, that number had increased to 9.8 hours! Moreover, the average adult is exposed to 362 ads per day.

Consider something for a minute. When was the last time you saw an advertisement encouraging you to *create* something? It shouldn't be difficult. You've seen more than 132,000 ads in the past year alone. I asked myself this question and couldn't think of a single example. Sure, Home Depot tells me I should take on more renovation projects, but that is still predicated on me first *buying* a product.

Even though the most successful people are creators, we're taught that consuming things is the true path to success. It's why Lincoln commercials feature Matthew Mcconaughey and Axe ads feature beautiful women. The message is always the same: buy this product and become a better version of yourself. In truth, our consumption makes *creators* successful.

To demonstrate this phenomena, I created a scale of consumption which places people, metaphorically, in a world where pure consumption and pure production are theoretically possible.

SCALE OF CONSUMPTION

PURE CONSUMER   PURE CREATOR

To the extreme left, we have someone who consumes everything and creates nothing. She wakes up, eats breakfast, watches TV, eats lunch, reads a magazine, watches more TV, eats dinner, and goes to sleep. She doesn't have a job because that would mean creating value for others.

To the extreme right, we have someone who creates everything and consumes nothing. She wakes up, makes breakfast for her family with food she grew herself, bikes to work at a company she started, spends all her time at work creating value for others, bikes back to the home she designed and built, cooks dinner for her kids, and goes to sleep.

The description of the pure creator sounds admittedly farfetched. What's interesting, however, is that the description of the pure consumer does not. In fact, you can probably think of someone who pretty closely matches that description.

If you're looking to be more successful in life, you may do so by increasing your production and decreasing your consumption. The same holds true for startups and companies. Most products and services exist because their creators have successfully convinced people to consume them. The more people you influence, the more successful you become.

Here's a helpful formula to help you along the way. Try to stay in the positive.

Hours spent producing + dollars made
- Hours spent consuming + dollars spent
_____

= **Net Production Score**

IDEAS

The Idea

Downplaying ideas is a growing trend in the startup universe. Everywhere you turn, you hear the adage "Ideas are worthless. It's all about execution!" I'm intimately familiar with this saying because I've voiced it countless times. I've sat in client meetings with entrepreneurs demanding an NDA and smiled kindly while I questioned their judgement. While NDAs are ridiculous, I disagree with the notion that ideas are worthless. Ideas are surprisingly valuable, just not in the way you might think.

Here's a quick thought experiment. Think of an idea for a startup, and pretend that idea is an egg. If you agreed with the notion that ideas are worthless, your egg would be worthless. Eggs in their raw state have little immediate value, but when cooked or combined with other ingredients, they become delicious. What's more, eggs represent an eventual chicken. That means eggs are tremendously valuable to their mother hens.

Like eggs, ideas are tremendously valuable to their creators. The problem is that entrepreneurs, unlike the hen, don't always know how to turn their ideas into startups. If the process of moving from idea to startup were predictable and known, ideas would be some of the most valuable assets in the world. Just imagine what people could create if we removed the fear and uncertainty of creation.

Rather than promoting the notion that ideas are worthless, we should direct our focus to breaking down barriers to creation. Our goal should be to make ideas more valuable, not to promote entrepreneurship as an exclusive club for those who know how to execute.

Customer Discovery

Customer discovery is the process of identifying, empathizing with, and learning from people in your target market to craft a better product or company. I won't get into the ins and outs of how to proper manage the customer discovery process. Frankly, there's an ocean of content online and dozens of free courses you can take to help you. This book is about going from idea to startup, and customer discovery is but a single tool in your startup shed.

To keep things brief, here's a quick summary of best practices when meeting with a prospective customer:

1. **Don't lead the witness.** Ask questions to uncover problems, not validate your idea.

2. **Document everything.** Write down responses to questions, take notes on interesting ideas, and look for patterns that may lead to validation.

3. **Stay in touch.** Customer discovery may result in actual customers when you launch your product. Keep them posted on your progress.

4. **Try to disprove your idea.** Make an effort to find reasons why no one would be interested in using your product. When you can no longer think of a reason, or your list is very short, you may have found something worthwhile.

Popular opinion in the startup universe dictates that you should always go through customer discovery, and I believe that's true for most founders. The problem arises when people blindly follow this advice without critical thought. Traditional customer discovery can take months to complete as you meet with people and document their feedback. This process is especially inefficient when your startup solves a problem you've personally experienced.

When I started Tenrocket, I had a deep understanding of the problem I was driven to solve. The pain of trying to launch a technology company and failing multiple times was so great that it was becoming detrimental to my marriage. I was so pissed off that I *had* to do something about it.

As it turns out, being pissed off about a problem is an excellent way to validate its efficacy. On a scale of 1 to 10, with 10 being the most pissed off you've ever been, anything beyond an 8 represents a potentially viable business opportunity. For example, my wife and I have documented that Comcast is slowly removing channels from our subscription package over the past six months. I don't need to set up a coffee meeting with a male aged 18-35 to know how annoying and soul-sucking that feels.

If you're not pissed off about the problem you're trying to solve, you're probably starting your business for one of three reasons:

1. You're extremely passionate about an industry
2. You're chasing money
3. You want to be an entrepreneur

In my experience, most idea stage entrepreneurs fall into one of these categories. You might be reading this and telling yourself that you're different, but the odds say otherwise. More than 300 entrepreneurs pitched me their ideas in 2015, and fewer than 20 were extremely pissed off about the problem they were trying to solve.

Assuming you do fall into one of the three categories above, traditional customer discovery is an option for you to consider. Another option is a much faster approach, which I recommend to everyone (even the pissed off founders).

Make a sale.

Let's make up another hypothetical startup and run it through the traditional customer discovery process. Then we'll take that same startup and try to make a sale.

Mike is extremely passionate about beer and loves collecting labels. In fact, he's saved the label of every new beer he's tried for the past three years. The problem is that Mike frequently tries new beers on draft. Without a label, how will Mike show the world an accurate number of the interesting craft brews he's tried?

Mike decides to launch BrewLabel, a new app which makes it easy for beer lovers to keep track of all the beers they've tried. You can even write tasting notes and rank the beers!

Traditional Customer Discovery

Mike Googles 'beer industry statistics' and finds that craft beer is a $19.6 billion market growing at an annual rate of 22%. Even better, Millennials represent the largest customer segment.

A millennial himself, Mike sets up eight meetings with 25-34 year-olds over the next two months. At each interview, he makes a point to ask the right questions, document the answers, and attempt to invalidate his idea. While every interviewee loved craft beer, Mike only found one person who shared his love of tracking the brews they've tried.

Mike goes back to the drawing board. While only one person enjoyed keeping track of beers, 6 of 8 followed their favorite breweries on social media. He reasons that if BrewLabel is going to work, it must somehow tap into these social networks. Mike decides that his app will allow people to login with Facebook and immediately get a list of all the breweries they follow. That way, everyone starts with a certain number of beers already checked off.

Mike schedules a new round of interviews aimed at diving deeper into how people follow breweries on social media. Over the next two months, he meets with ten new Millennials and documents their responses. This time, only four report that they follow breweries they like on Facebook. Not bad, but not as promising as the first round of interviews.

Mike continues this process for another month and ultimately uncovers a problem faced by more than 50% of his interviewees: craft beer lovers want to try new beers, but they have trouble deciding between so many similar options.

There are *thousands* of IPAs on the market. How does one choose between them? Mike pivots and decides to solve this problem. His app will be the Netflix of Beer!

Making a Sale

Mike goes to launchrock.com and builds a simple landing page for BrewLabel in a few hours. He includes a large 'Download from AppStore' button near the top, which opens a popup when clicked letting prospective users know that the app is coming shortly. To sign up for the waiting list, they submit their name and email.

Mike posts a link to his new landing page in several online craft beer communities, including a detailed description of the problem he's faced and why he's driven to solve it. With Launchrock's built-in analytics tool, Mike can track the number of unique page views, button clicks, and form submissions on his new landing page. Over the next few days, Mike sees that his page has 426 unique visitors. Of those visitors, 70 clicked the button to download the app. Of those 70 people, 48 filled out the form and signed up for the waiting list. From this data, Mike gathers that his idea for BeerLabel can capture an estimated 11% conversion rate (48/426) from visitors to his landing page.

While BrewLabel is still at the idea stage, Mike was able to convince 11% of his target market to visit his website and ultimately download his app. Rather than spending months asking people to describe their needs, he spent an afternoon building a website and letting people know about his product. It wouldn't be wise for Mike to invest thousands of dollars after one basic test, but the test itself is easily repeatable. In just a few short weeks, Mike can identify additional craft brew communities and tweak his messaging to increase conversions.

Tenrocket started when I pitched the concept to a room of fifteen early stage entrepreneurs at an event in Atlanta. After my pitch, a founder in the room raised his hand and said: "I'll do that". He became my first customer even before

I had an actual product. If you have people demanding your product before it's even a real thing, you know you're on to something.

Legal

We've already covered my disdain for NDAs earlier in the book. Sadly, it's just the tip of the iceberg when it comes to legal advice for startups. One need only search Google to find a barrage of legal advice for entrepreneurs, ranging from "How to incorporate your startup" to "Why you should file your patent ASAP".

I'm not one to suggest that all legal advice for startups is BS. On the contrary, I've learned that having excellent attorneys with an understanding of your business is one of the most substantial assets you can have as a founder. What bothers me is that most thought leaders in the legal services sector fail to acknowledge the *stage* of a founder's business. Rarely do you find mention of idea stage legal advice, and when you do, lawyers have a vested interest in convincing you to seek protection. There's something fundamentally wrong with coaxing an entrepreneur at the idea stage into filing a provisional patent when he hasn't built a product. This 'first to file' mentality is a fear-driven approach. "What happens if someone else steals my idea?" Lawyers know this, and the bad ones take advantage.

I incorporated Tenrocket retroactively after already being in business for three months. I once thought of this as stupidity, but then again, I had incorporated two ideas in prior years that never became startups or businesses. With Tenrocket, I had my first customer before even starting.

I'm not an attorney, and none of this advice should be considered anything beyond that of a founder sharing his perspective on a complex matter. Still, I have a general rule of thumb for navigating the legal world as a startup founder.

1. If you don't have a product, customers, or anything proprietary, it's too early to incorporate or seek legal assistance.

2. If you have a product but lack customers or anything proprietary, incorporate.

3. If you have something proprietary but lack product or customers, seek legal assistance.

4. If you have customers but lack product or anything proprietary, incorporate.

In all cases, remember that attorneys have something to gain by convincing you to protect yourself and your idea. If legal consideration is preventing you from building product or making sales, you're probably wasting your time.

PRODUCT

Design

Fans of the Pixar movie UP will probably remember Dug, the lovable dog who just wanted to please his master. Dug was a good boy who loved to play, but he would frequently get distracted mid-sentence and yell out, "Squirrel!". He'd then carry on his conversation as if nothing happened.

I meet with entrepreneurs on daily, sometimes hourly basis, and you'd be amazed at how similar they are to Doug when it comes to design. Founders are obsessed with beautiful, shiny objects. This love of design is put on hyperdrive when it comes to our ideas. Though we lack formal design training, suddenly we all become experts when our future company is on the line.

Don't get me wrong - design is a critical consideration in the long-term success of a company. My beef with beautiful design is when entrepreneurs consider it a 'must-have' for their idea. It's not enough for us to simply make our ideas a reality. They're our *babies*, and we can't have an ugly baby.

Modern technology makes it amazingly easy to get fantastic design without knowing how to use Photoshop or write software. Tools like Webflow, Invision, and Principle are democratizing the design process, and sites like Awwwards make it easy to model your design after industry best practices. If you must wrap a pretty red bow around your startup idea, please use one of these tools before paying a designer thousands of dollars to do it for you.

Of course, my advice is to avoid the red bow, at least until your concept crosses *The Real Gap* and becomes a real startup. Design at the idea stage is a distraction. It tells me that you care more about perfecting your idea than executing on it. Just look at Craigslist. By industry standards, it's a horrible design. The entire site greets users with excessive text written in Times New Roman font and blue underlined links. Yet somehow, despite the eyesore, Craigslist is still the go-to classified marketplace online. How do they do it? By solving a specific problem very well, staying focused on what they do best, and executing on a consistent user adoption strategy.

Think of design as your reward for actually building or selling your idea. Your first users will be so thrilled about the problem you're solving; they won't care about how shiny your product looks. These people are called early adopters, and you should do everything in your power to make their lives awesome (more on that later). Once you convince enough early adopters to buy your product, it might be a good time to reward yourself with a simple design upgrade. Until then, stay heads down on product and sales.

Development

Product development is perhaps the most misunderstood component of launching a startup. As the founder of Tenrocket, product is very near and dear to my heart. It's the number one thing I see founders screw up the most, and the problem is that it's almost entirely not their fault.

If you're capable of taking an idea and transforming it into a product yourself, you probably haven't felt the pain of what we'll call the non-technical founder. Non-technical founders tend to be sales and leadership driven, inspiring people with their vision for the future. Sadly, despite their positive presence, they often lack the fundamental skill required to make that vision a reality. That's where developers come in.

Great developers are like giant squid. We know they exist, but finding one in the wild is nearly impossible. Non-tech entrepreneurs frequently embark on elaborate quests to find great developers and become so enamored by the journey that they lose sight of the destination. When they finally manage to meet a great developer, it's like finally talking to that hot colleague you've had a secret crush on for years. They geek out, appear needy, and neglect to be themselves. It's not that great developers don't exist, it's just that it's damned near impossible to find and land one. There's a surprisingly rational reason for this: great developers don't need you.

Great developers have it *made*. They possess a skill that seems so magical they routinely land six-figure salaries with flexible hours and cushy benefits. Take a minute to picture yourself as a great developer with this kind of life. Now imagine getting an email from someone you've never met requesting a meeting to chat though his "disruptive idea that will revolutionize the (insert huge sector) industry." Sounds crazy right? It happens every day.

Let's take it a step further and say you meet this founder to hear him out. If he's like most idea stage founders, he'll probably pitch you on becoming his co-founder. He may not talk about equity just yet, but I'd wager the average deal is 30-50% equity for a full-time commitment, 10% for simply building the product.

Take a moment and consider the ridiculousness of this request. Two people meet for the first time and have no idea what it's like to work together. They are about to embark on a venture with a 90% risk of failure and an estimated capital expense of $50,000 in the first year. Either one of these guys could be an ax murderer, but neither would know because most co-founders don't run background checks on each other. Imagine going out for coffee on a first date and having the other person ask for your hand in marriage. That's how great developers feel when being pitched co-founder roles by non-tech founders.

Fortunately, there is a way to land a technical co-founder, and it's pretty straightforward. About three months after I started Tenrocket, my good friend Justin Richards showed up on my floor at Atlanta Tech Village. He had just quit his job at Turner Broadcasting to pursue a startup idea he'd been working on for two years. A skilled programmer, Justin was financing himself by taking freelance coding gigs for startups on the side.

I had known Justin for almost a year and had a very solid

understanding of who he was. When I moved from Augusta to Atlanta in late 2013, Justin was the first friend I made. We met at a local event where he was pitching his new startup, Kio - a platform connecting businesses with local designers. I remember being very impressed with Justin, but had some pretty blunt feedback about Kio. Rather than avoiding me or getting defensive, Justin came up to me afterward to say thanks for being honest. He's one of those rare people who can take criticism, improve upon himself, and come out the other side without taking it personally.

As it turns out, the day Justin showed up on my floor was the day I began my search for a co-founder at Tenrocket. Given our friendship, knowledge of each others strengths, and shared passion for innovation, I pitched him on a week-long trial to be my co-founder. He gave it some thought and ultimately accepted, nailing the trial the next week.

When seeking a co-founder, technical or otherwise, there are three things you should always do:

Ask for advice.

Asking for advice proves that you value the other person's opinion and respect her time. Instead of pitching a great developer on becoming your technical co-founder, ask questions. "Which software language is best for my startup?" "How long should this take an experienced developer?" If the developer is interested in becoming your founder, she may bring it up herself. More likely, she'll see you as a driven, considerate entrepreneur who isn't desperate to find help.

Build a relationship.

Meet with this person frequently as a friend, always making sure to offer your help before asking for hers. As you get to know one another, you'll pick up critical insight about personality, stress tolerance, work habits, and personal passions.

Set clear expectations.

Define roles, establish equity share (50/50 is my recommendation, assuming you're both full-time), decide who gets the final say in decisions, agree on how the business (and yourselves) will be funded, and build a basic plan to make your idea a reality. Save things like culture and branding for later discussion.

Agencies

Of course, finding a technical co-founder is only one option for moving from idea to startup. Another option is working with an agency, which I define as a company of five or more employees building technical products in-house for others. Famous agencies like HUGE and Hello Monday have hundreds of employees spread all over the world, enrolling big-name clients like Coca-Cola, Nike, and Disney.

Without a doubt, agencies build some of the most beautiful software products known to man. Most of the work you see on design award websites was probably handcrafted by teams of designers, developers, and brand experts at these agencies. They are the Rolls Royce of technical product builders. Every detail is meticulously accounted for, down to the pixel.

The problem with agencies is that, like the Rolls Royce, the beautiful products they create have outrageously large price tags. Depending on the agency, an app can range from $50,000 to $250,000 and beyond. Remember the very minimal app I built in ten days after three months of coding education? The cheapest quote I ever received to build it was $25,000. That quote was from a dev shop, which is like an agency but with a much smaller team (usually 2-5 guys). Both times I called a major agency, the quote exceeded six figures. At the time, I made $42,000 a year as a nonprofit fundraising professional.

You may be thinking to yourself, "Man, working with an agency sounds amazing! I wish I could afford to hire one."

You're *partially* right. Working with agencies is an incredible experience, and they do roll out the red carpet for their clients. For corporations working on major products seen by millions of people, this totally makes sense. For startup founders, especially those at the idea stage, it's one of the worst decisions you could ever make.

It's not that agencies are the bad guys. They do fantastic work that inspires others and makes the world a better place. I'm pro-agency. In fact, many agencies wish they were able to help more startups. The problem stems from their high cost of overhead. Agencies employ some of the world's most brilliant creative minds, and those minds don't come cheap.

If you consider a typical large agency with 250 employees, each earning an average of $50,000 per year, you wind up with an annual salary expense of $12.5 million dollars. Add in the cost of benefits, utilities, computers, software, lawyers, and space to house those employees, and it becomes easy to see why these companies charge so much. That same agency would have to take on 250 projects at $50k each to make up for employee salaries alone. Assuming the average project takes three months to complete (which is generous), they would need to squeeze in more than 60 projects per quarter to hit that mark.

Armed with this knowledge, I can't help but smile when I think back on pitching an agency with an equity opportunity as an idea-stage founder. At the time, I truly believed they were missing out on a golden opportunity to invest a little time into something that would change the world. I simply didn't understand that they needed dozens of paying clients just to make ends meet for their employees.

But what if your financial circumstances are different? What if you recently ran into a healthy amount of cash, perhaps through inheritance or investment. Should you work with an agency?

NO.

Throwing tons of money at ideas is almost never a good plan, much less so when you're spending someone else's money. For whatever reason, money (especially investment) tends to poison our brains, tricking us into thinking we're on to something big. When it comes to spending six figures on a new product, there's a monumental difference when comparing a corporate buyer with an idea or startup. That difference? **Customers**. Lots of them.

If you know beyond a shadow of a doubt that millions or even hundreds of thousands of people will see and use your product within three months of launch, it might be a good idea to work with an agency. For the sake of this book, we'll call this strategy *The Hail Mary*. Millions of people are counting on a single play, so you better make sure it's a good one.

The alternative to *The Hail Mary* is simpler, more flexible, and far less expensive. We'll call this strategy, *The Grind*.

The Grind is the opposite of *The Hail Mary*. Rather than banking everything on the success of a single play, *The Grind* is about strategically designing a series of smaller plays with the goal of incrementally learning and improving throughout the game. If mistakes are made along the way, *The Grind* allows you to learn from those errors and design new experiments to eliminate them.

If this sounds familiar, it might be because it's remarkably similar to the scientific method. In the startup universe, this concept is often referred to as lean startup methodology. While we won't take a deep dive into lean startup principles in this book, you can pick up a copy of Eric Ries' *The Lean Startup* to explore the concept further.

How does this relate to agencies and products? Simple. As a non-tech founder looking to get an idea off the ground, you can either start with *The Hail Mary* or *The Grind*. We already know that working with an agency is the foundational play of The Hail Mary strategy, but what about *The Grind*?

With agencies off the table, we're left with four options. To continue the metaphor, let's consider them players you can draft to your startup team. The only exception? You can only pick one. How you make the choice comes down to risk tolerance, budget, and time.

1. The co-founder
2. The dev shop
3. The freelancer
4. The freelance marketplace

The co-founder

As you may have guessed, finding a co-founder is the least expensive option. Most people make the assumption that because it's the cheapest option, and because most investors don't invest in solo-founder ventures, it's also the least *risky* option. What people fail to acknowledge is a third consideration: time. While co-founders are inexpensive, the time investment it takes to find a good one is substantial. You should expect to spend at least three months building the relationship AFTER you've found and met the person. It's remarkably similar to the dynamics of a good marriage. Look for a long time, meet someone you like, date, propose, marry. In startups, many founders people jump straight to the last step. That's an incredibly risky move.

When should you seek the co-founder option?

1. You've already built a solid relationship with an amazing developer.

2. You've asked that developer for advice about your startup, and she's expressed interest in the idea.

3. You're confident she can finish the first version of you product within a three-month timeframe.

The dev shop

If you don't already know an amazing developer who has expressed interest in your idea, you might consider finding a dev shop to build your product. Dev shops are product development teams comprised of 2-5 people, usually with a focus on technology. You'll likely find several dev shops with just two or three employees. A very common scenario is one developer, one designer, and one administrator. Dev shops typically range in price from $10-50k per project, with the goal of promoting an agency experience without the agency price.

Dev shops span a wide range of cost, risk, and timeliness of delivery. In my experience, the good ones have a solid administrator on staff to keep projects running smoothly and make sure client needs are considered first. While the bad shops may have strong technical skills, they tend to lack client empathy, project management skills, and a general business sense.

When should you consider the dev shop option?

1. You either don't have an existing relationship with an amazing developer, or do, but she's not interested or available.

2. The dev shop in question has a very solid reputation, which you've confirmed by speaking with several of their clients.

3. The dev shop in question has said no to one or more features, asked very detailed questions about your product and company, explained their work process in detail, has appeared very organized in their work and communication with you, and asked questions to make sure you're the right client for them.

The freelancer

You know the saying about how even bad pizza is pretty good? Freelancers aren't like that. Working with a bad freelancer is one of the most frustrating experiences in the entire world. I'd rank it right alongside a customer service call with Comcast, only imagine that call costing thousands of dollars and taking place over several months.

On the other hand, working with a great freelancer is one of the *best* feelings in the world. Somehow they 'just get you' and make everything seem easy. Like dev shops, freelancers vary considerably in price, risk, and timeliness of delivery. I work with freelancers every day who repeatedly blow me away with their speed, intellect, and drive. These guys live and breathe creativity and take pride in their work. It's like art to them. That's the kind of freelancer you want to hire.

So how do you find one? We'll discuss that in a later section. For now, here's when you should consider hiring a freelancer:

1. The freelancer in question is extremely detail-oriented, insisting that project expectations, scope of work, and contractual obligations are discussed in detail before agreeing to get started.

2. The freelancer has an online portfolio of work so you can see, download, and interact with products she has built.

3. The freelancer willingly provides contact information for former clients so you can check references.

4. You have a good feeling about this freelancer, her integrity, and her understanding of your product.

The freelance marketplace

Freelance marketplaces are online platforms connecting clients with contract workers. While the result of working with a freelancer is the same as hiring one directly, platforms offer additional benefits that mirror what you might get from an agency or dev shop - things like project management, built-in contracts, third party review, quality assurance, and consultation.

You might think working with a freelance marketplace provides some assurance that the project will go well, but sadly, that is not always the case. While most of the larger marketplaces have thousands, sometimes millions of freelancers, they do a poor job of managing quality and customer empathy at scale. There are several factors at work here, but two stand out in my mind. First, the largest freelance marketplaces know that they must compete on price. They allow freelancers to set whatever price they wish for their time, creating a race to the bottom where the cheapest freelancer wins out. Despite the prevalence of review systems and comments, these freelancers continuously earn work and churn out more and more disappointing projects.

The second factor reducing quality at scale is the lack of curation of freelance talent. Rather than handpicking the world's best freelancers, large marketplaces allow anyone to sign up and market their services. You can go online right now, sign up as a developer on one of these marketplaces, copy some pretty screenshots from google images, and upload them to your profile as examples of work. Get a few friends to write glowing reviews, and you're well on your way to getting your first client.

Thankfully, freelance marketplaces aren't all bad. The great ones have a surprising amount in common and gain a bit more traction every day as more people flee the horrible customer experience of the larger marketplaces. As you might imagine, the best marketplaces care a lot about the quality of work produced by their talent pool. They have measures in place to ensure customers are delivered a great product, and the elite marketplaces go as far as to offer a money-back guarantee if expectations aren't met. Great marketplaces understand that their success as a company stems from having the best freelance talent in their community. Predictably, they average a 5-10% acceptance rate for prospective freelancers applying to join. On of my favorite freelancers at Tenrocket is a former IBM developer specifically hired to churn out rapid prototypes for their best ideas.

When should you hire a freelance marketplace?

1. The marketplace handpicks and stands by its quality of freelance talent.

2. The marketplace offers a money-back guarantee on projects that are not delivered to expectation.

3. The marketplace has a commitment to outstanding customer support, answering your questions in a timely and detailed manner.

4. The marketplace provides examples of work and offers to connect you with former clients for reference.

5. The marketplace is very transparent and upfront with it's pricing and timeline.

6. You feel confident that both the marketplace (most will assign you a project manager) and the freelancer understand you, your product, and your needs extremely well.

7. There is a clear game plan for moving forward after the initial product is built.

8. The marketplace has a price floor (minimum price on categories of projects - ex. app development) to eliminate the race-to-the-bottom pricing strategy of many larger competitors.

In all cases, from co-founder to freelance marketplace, the single most important thing you can do to set your product on the right track is outline expectations in very clear detail from the beginning. Anyone building your product should be adamant about discussing the finer points, documenting expectations, clearly outlining a scope of work, and describing the path forward. She should have a genuine interest in your work, instill a sense of honesty (even if that honesty is brutal at times), and promote a feeling of togetherness and shared responsibility.

Iterations & Pivots

Ideas and products are almost never Hail Mary passes. Perhaps the biggest lie surrounding startups is this notion of the inspirational founder who conjures an idea from some magical moment, builds a team around that idea, and overcomes tremendous obstacles to bring that idea to mass adoption. In practice, entrepreneurs are typically wrong about their assumptions at first. The big idea you have in your head as you read this probably won't work out.

What separates successful entrepreneurs from idea people is the ability to iterate and pivot their ideas, startups, and companies. Utilizing a process very similar to the scientific method, they are obsessive about testing hypothesis, running experiments, analyzing the results, and implementing new discoveries. As we improve incrementally, we become more likely to make big discoveries that are later perceived as overnight successes.

Peter Thiel suggests in his book Zero to One that the world is so caught up in incremental improvements that we neglect to take monumental leaps forward as a society. He proposes having a big idea, building an amazing team and culture around that idea, and aligning every effort into actualizing that vision. It's an inspiring read and a welcome debate in opposition to books like Eric Ries' The Lean Startup.

The problem is that most people are not instinctively capable of being zero to one entrepreneurs, at least not at first. We can all certainly become one, but the process takes time. One of my core struggles as an entrepreneur is the temptation of comparing myself to other, more successful founders. I've discovered that most early-stage founders share in this struggle with me. We look at people like Elon Musk and think "How can I someday become more like him? What special sauce does he have that I'm somehow missing?"

When we make those comparisons, we neglect to realize a few very important distinctions. We make assumptions about these entrepreneurial superstars and place them on pedestals of greatness without truly understanding the sacrifice, pain, and even the process of getting there. One of Peter Thiel's most foundational beliefs is that the world's most transformational companies are built on secrets - something an entrepreneur knows to be true that most people disagree with him on. If we take a careful look at the startup sector as a whole, I believe one of the biggest secrets is that successful entrepreneurs are scientists masquerading as business people.

The problem is that most scientific discoveries are shared, metaphorically, in two versions: peer-reviewed journals and magazine articles. The vast majority of the world chooses to read magazine articles instead of peer-reviewed journals. In doing this, we neglect to understand the agonizing detail and failed experiments that led, sometimes over years, to a breakthrough. We simply read headlines like "Apple reinvents the phone" and build the founder up to some form of demigod. That founder is then incentivized to promote this narrative because it's not a bad thing for your competition to think you have superpowers. It also makes for a great recruiting tool.

For the *world* to move from zero to one, more *people* have to move from zero to one. For more people to move from zero to one, more *ideas* need to move from zero to one. Most people will never attend an Ivy League university or start the next Apple. The world is full of smart people stuck in boring office jobs who dream of bringing an idea to life. Whether or not that idea will go on to revolutionize an industry isn't the point. The point is getting that person to leave the boring office job, pursue a worthy challenge, and do so in a way that minimizes her risk of failure. Collectively this will build a more entrepreneurial world of people capable of and confident in pursuing bold, ambitious ideas.

MARKETING

Most failures in idea stage marketing can be traced back to a lack of focus, inconsistency of message, high expense, and failure to measure. Marketing should never take precedence over product and sales at the idea stage, and it should rarely be considered at all. That being said, marketing done well will generate tremendous insight from your target audience, which can be useful for iterating upon your concept and adjusting your message to achieve more sales.

Pitching

The very first component of marketing to get right at the idea stage is your pitch. People tend to think of pitches as inspiring speeches you give in front of a room full of investors, and that scares them. In reality, a pitch is simply a 30-second(ish) response to the question "What do you do?" It's ironic to consider the hours, days and months idea-stage entrepreneurs invest into their ideas, only to flounder when asked to describe them at a high level.

Since landing our first Tenrocket client at an Atlanta event called Pitch Practice back in summer 2014, I've had the pleasure of hearing more than 300 pitches. The founders have ranged from just starting out with their first idea to serial entrepreneurs with millions in the bank. One entrepreneur had been on an episode of Shark Tank and received investment from Mark Cuban. He was *still* practicing.

Idea-stage entrepreneurs, especially those pitching for the first time, tend to make very predictable mistakes in their pitch. Assuming that people won't understand the concept, they often go into extreme detail, describing core processes and business models that frankly have no relevance to the listener. On the contrary, experienced entrepreneurs have a knack for quickly and effectively getting to the point. Steve Jobs was famous for coming up with 'Twitter-ready' headlines that were easily repeatable, shareable, and consistent. While most of us remember the iPod tagline "a thousand songs in your pocket", we probably wouldn't remember "a portable MP3 player with a beautiful user interface, ten hours of battery life, and a scroll wheel for browsing songs". Laugh all you want, but most idea-stage entrepreneurs go into even more detail than that.

Our pitch at Tenrocket has been simple and easy to remember from the beginning, and that was very much by design.

"We build apps for startups in ten days for $10k".

We modify this pitch and frequently make it a bit longer or more inspirational depending on the audience, but that's always the one thing people remember about us. I've been at startup events and overheard other people deliver our pitch to their friends. It's consistent, easy to remember, and cuts out the typical 'look at me' sales-pitch that plagues most entrepreneurs.

Working alongside Kevin Sandlin, the creator of Pitch Practice, I've been fortunate enough to see him create a formula for delivering an effective startup pitch. The thing I love most about this formula is that it's agnostic of time. You can use it to deliver a 30-second elevator pitch, elaborate on each category for a 5-minute pitch, or make a full blown 20-30 minute presentation in front of a crowd. Here's the rundown:

1. Name and company name
2. Problem
3. Solution
4. Customer
5. Ask

Kevin also recommends watching Start With Why - an amazing TED Talk given by Simon Sinek - to effectively communicate the problem you're solving. This formula is a fantastic starting point, and writing down your answers is completely ok (even encouraged), at first. Remember our friend Kyle and his idea for Kreemy - the Uber of ice cream? Let's see if we can craft a pitch using Kevin's pitch formula.

"My name is Kyle, and my company is called Kreemy (name and company name). When I was a kid, the best feeling in the world was hearing the sound of an ice cream truck roll through my neighborhood. Sadly, I'm an adult now, and I can't remember the last time I heard that sound (problem). That's why I founded Kreemy. Kreemy delivers ice cream at the push of a button (solution). So if you're an ice cream lover like me (customer), simply download the app, press a button, and an ice cream man will show up in 15 minutes or less (ask)."

The great thing about this pitch is it can be shortened or lengthened as needed. Say Kyle attends a noisy party, and a friend asks him what he's been up to lately. Kyle replies: "I started a company called Kreemy. We deliver ice cream at the push of a button." There's no way in hell that guy isn't asking a follow-up question, and that is precisely the goal of an effective pitch. Always tell just enough to hook their interest, but leave enough out to spark their curiosity. You want people thinking "How in the world does he do that?"

Branding

Quick, what's Instagram's brand strategy?

Unless you work at Instagram, you probably have no clue. Don't feel bad. Most people could repeat the same question with some of the world's most famous brands - even their favorites - and have no idea. Pixar is my favorite company in the world, but I couldn't tell you their brand strategy to save my life.

People make the mistake of looking at successful companies and believing those companies are successful because of their branding. We see things like 'Think Different' by Apple or Nike's famous swoosh logo and believe that our startups must have equally awesome branding to succeed. In reality, branding is probably the last thing you should worry about as an idea-stage entrepreneur.

Obvious as it may sound, successful branding requires that

you have brand recognition. Nike is a global corporation with millions of customers, so effective branding is a critical component of their marketing strategy. If they don't brand themselves effectively, they might easily lose market share to Reebok, Adidas, or Under Armour. Even a 1% change in market share at that level is considered extremely damaging.

The *opposite* is true for idea-stage founders. Focusing on things like your company name, logo, and brand personality means time is taken away from product development and sales. Building your brand at the idea stage is like building a Tesla chassis around a skateboard, and even *that* is a bit generous. Skateboards are still a functional product.

I'm not suggesting you neglect branding altogether. Having a company name is part of your pitch, and a logo will add legitimacy to your idea when people dig deeper. The problem arises when branding becomes the major focus and prevents entrepreneurs from focusing on more important tasks. I recently met an early-stage entrepreneur who spent $65,000 on branding before launch. Regardless of whether or not he succeeds, that's just ridiculous.

My business partner and I became so fed up with this branding obsession that last year, we created a workshop titled, "How to Launch your Startup in 20 minutes". In that 20 minutes, we created a fictitious startup idea from scratch, named that startup, created a logo, and built a landing page that we could send to prospective customers. We even had time left over to discuss a social media strategy. It seems like magic, but it's actually pretty straightforward. In fact, you can do it right now. We created a video back in November 2015 to make the whole process extremely easy to understand. It's a visual process, so watching the video as you go along will be helpful. Before you start, go ahead and sign up for Google Drive (drive.google.com). We're big fans of getting things out the door, so please excuse the less-than-perfect production quality.

How To Launch a Startup in 20 Minutes
https://youtu.be/fqjTW_igxQQ

Measurement

There's a reason most entrepreneurs neglect to measure and track their experiments - it can get extremely boring. We're not all scientists by nature, and the idea of going back to the lab reminds us more of high school chemistry than becoming a startup rockstar. Something you should know about real life startup rockstars is they're freaking obsessive about measurement. They look at growth as a game of Super Mario Brothers, and every point gained gets them that much closer to storming Bowser's Castle. You may be at the idea stage, but that doesn't mean you can afford to neglect to measure and analyze your experiments.

Consider the Kreemy app idea. Though it may be just an idea, there's a lot of work required to validate its legitimacy. We can run through a traditional customer discovery process and painstakingly document responses from potential users. That's one option, and it's certainly viable. We could also send the landing page to a bunch of potential users, monitoring page views, tracking click-through rates, and ultimately capturing conversion metrics along the way.

What you want to avoid is being the 'ballpark' guy, who looks at metrics as something to get close rather than know precisely. You might think, "what's the difference if I'm a few percentage points off?" From a pure numbers perspective, you're right. An estimated conversion rate of 10% versus an actual conversion rate of 13% isn't that big a deal, especially when we're talking about idea validation.

The problem is that those ballpark numbers represent something deeper: a sloppy founder. Have you ever watched an episode of Shark Tank where the guy pitching doesn't know his numbers? They rip these entrepreneurs to pieces, and it has a lot more to do with the not-knowing than the numbers themselves. If you're married, you know the importance of not ball-parking numbers. I know my anniversary is on October 23rd because it's important to me, and not knowing that number would make my wife upset. Be a good spouse to your startup and know your numbers.

Social Media

The best advice I can offer to idea-stage entrepreneurs pursuing social media as a marketing channel is to pick a single medium. It's easy to get caught up in the hype and post on every channel imaginable, but in practice, this can dilute your message and lead to a lack of focus. Consider your product and marketing, and try to choose the social platform that provides the best fit. Is your product more visually-driven? Instagram might be the right fit for you. Tech startups tend to do well on Twitter. Handmade goods are great for Pinterest.

Have you considered that you may not need to be on social media at all? Most people assume that social media is a must-have these days, but that's not the case for idea-stage founders. A good way to find out is by measuring your social media efforts to make sure they are effectively engaging your target audience. How many of your followers have converted to customers? How many share your content with others?

These are important numbers to know because every minute you spend on social media is a minute you could be spending on another marketing channel. If social is working for you, great! If not, consider one of the *many* other channels - even traditional ones - and try to craft inexpensive experiments where you can test their efficacy. For more on this experimental marketing methodology, pick up a fantastic book called *Traction* by Gabriel Weinberg and Justin Mares.

Growth

If you've already started experimenting with different marketing channels and measuring the results, you're half-way to an awesome growth strategy. The second half is finding and utilizing the right tools. I caution idea-stage entrepreneurs from becoming fixated on growth, much less growth strategy, but I think it's a good thing as long as you understand the risks. Making the decision to grow your idea or startup seems like a no-brainer to most people, but there is significant danger in growing too early or too fast. Just know that measurement is a growth hacker's best friend, and becoming obsessive about improving those metrics a little each day will add up much more quickly than you think.

MONEY

Investment

Back in 2014 when I was working to get my education app off the ground, I firmly believed I needed to find investment. Having just left a nonprofit consulting gig that turned out to be a total bust, I was completely broke. It was quite possibly the worst time to start a company.

I didn't realize it at the time, but my likelihood of getting investment was incredibly small, even as a professional fundraiser. It's not that I wasn't a good entrepreneur or that my idea sucked (although both of those things were true at the time), but something much more fundamental. As it turns out, there is a very predictable formula for getting investment, which I'll share with you below. First, we take a look at the components of an idea or startup.

Entrepreneur(s) - the person or people striving to build a successful company

Product - something created or refined for the purpose of sale

Traction - the extent to which a product gains popularity or acceptance.

INVESTABILITY FORMULA

$$\text{LIKELIHOOD OF RECEIVING INVESTMENT} = \frac{\text{ENTREPRENEUR} + \text{PRODUCT} + \text{TRACTION}}{10}$$

When running the formula, we assign each component a score from 1-10. Each point corresponds to a percentage rank of that component when compared to all others in the world. For example, Elon Musk would represent a level 10 entrepreneur. His company Tesla would also represent a level

42

10 product, and that product would have level 10 traction. It's virtually impossible for Tesla not to receive investment. At the low end of the equation are components that have yet to exist. An eight-year-old with an idea for a product and no sales would represent a level 1 entrepreneur, product, and traction.

Let's say Elon Musk were to start a brand new venture tomorrow (as if Tesla, SpaceX, and Solar City aren't keeping him busy enough). Elon is such a world class entrepreneur that - if needed - it would be almost impossible for him not to receive investment. Since he's a level 10 entrepreneur, his likelihood of investment is 10/10.

The same holds true for amazing products. Take the iPhone for example - a level 10 product. If the iPhone never existed and was introduced to the world today by that same eight-year-old, it's such a beautiful and revolutionary product that it would almost certainly get investment, despite the inexperience of its inventor.

Let's say that same eight-year-old had an idea for the iPhone and could explain in detail not only how it works, but how he would bring it to market. He hops on Kickstarter and makes an awesome explainer video introducing the world to the iPhone, and people go nuts. In just days his funding goal of $10,000 is surpassed.

A week goes by, and he's at $250,000. By the time his campaign closes after 30 days, he raises $8 million - one of the most successful Kickstarter campaigns of all time. All he needs to do now is build a bunch of iPhones and fulfill the orders. With $8 million in pre-sales, this kid would be a virtual lock for additional investment.

If you look closely, reading the examples above uncovers an interesting trend. Even though Elon Musk, the kid who built the iPhone, and the kid who started the Kickstarter campaign are virtual locks for investment, you could make the argument that none of them technically need it. Elon Musk has a ton of money himself, why would he need investment?

The kid who built the iPhone may not have money or sales, but the iPhone sells itself. The kid who started the Kickstarter campaign now has $8 million in seed funding from pre-sales to fulfill orders. Each of these entrepreneurs has the freedom to take investment or not, and that's a beautiful feeling.

Of course, most of us are not Elon Musk. We don't have iPhone-quality products developed or $8 million in pre-sales. As much as we'd like to put ourselves at a level 5 or higher entrepreneur, the reality is that anyone at that level or higher has probably started a successful company already. Additionally, every point gained represents an exponentially more difficult step. It's easy to move from a level 1 entrepreneur to a level 2, but it's twice as hard to move from 2 to 3. Same goes for product and sales.

In seeking investment at the idea stage, most entrepreneurs fail for a very simple reason - they're not investable. You might be a level 3 entrepreneur (the equivalent of a world-class developer or salesman with a great idea), but without product or traction, you stand a pretty small chance of getting investment on the merits of your idea alone. It makes sense when you think about it - why would a world-class developer with a great idea not have built a working version of his product already? If his idea is so great, why would the amazing salesman not have any pre-sales?

Think of your startup as a fire you're trying to build. If you're thinking of investment as a match to get the fire started, you're too early. Investment is much better utilized as gasoline to throw on existing fires and make them grow faster. If you throw gasoline on a pile of sticks, nothing happens. Ideas without products or sales are like piles of sticks to investors.

If you can afford it, my recommendation is to avoid investment for as long as possible. The earlier you raise money, the more equity you'll give away. After I built my education app, an investor I admired offered me $15,000 in exchange for 50% equity. You might think that's a ridiculous offer, but in reality, my app was just a simple prototype with no sales. A $30,000 valuation was a reasonable offer. The fact that it had the potential to disrupt the education sector was of minimal importance, considering it had yet to disrupt a single student.

Of course, sometimes the money just isn't there. I know what it's like to have limited options. It's what inspired me to start Tenrocket in the first place. If you find yourself in a position where you need external funding to go from idea to startup, you have several options.

Option 1: Pre-sales

Selling your idea before it becomes a product is my absolute favorite way to fund a project. It requires you to do the hard work - selling something - before investing time into building it. Pre-sales work very well for service companies (dev shops, consultants, etc.), but with the advent of crowdfunding, it's also a fantastic strategy for physical products.

Crowdfunding is a bit trickier for software products, but you can still create a quick landing page to measure how many people click to download or sign up for your product. You can even pre-sell a free mobile app this way, with the goal of demonstrating enough traction to attract an investor or prospective co-founder.

Option 2: Build it yourself

If you're the business and marketing guy, you probably think product development is out of the question for you. Before I knew how to code, I certainly used to think this way. Coding has a bad reputation of being a math-driven, nerdy endeavor. In reality, I've discovered that coding is an incredibly creative pursuit and that the individual styles of programmers vary substantially. You don't have to be a math wizard or engineering major to learn how to build a product. You don't even have to enroll in an expensive coding academy like I did (although they certainly help to expedite the learning process). You can go online right now and find a bevy of free and inexpensive learning tools designed to help you learn how to build awesome products. Even if you have someone building your product for you, it doesn't hurt to have a working knowledge of the product development process, be it software or hardware. While there are dozens of websites and apps to choose from, my personal favorite is Treehouse (teamtreehouse.com).

Option 3: Get a job

Not everyone can afford to be a full-time entrepreneur, and that's totally ok. Keeping yourself and your family alive is far more important than any startup you could create, so it's important to keep things in perspective. If you're broke and don't have a job, your primary focus should be finding a way to make an income.

Some people have the luxury of living with their parents during this phase, but that's not predictable enough for me to recommend. I started Tenrocket while broke and jobless, but I also had my first client and a check in hand.

If you already have a job and are considering quitting to pursue your startup, my advice is to do so when you have a financial runway of 6 months or greater, or are so amazing at what you do that it would be incredibly easy for you to get re-hired if your startup fails.

Option 4: Sell everything

A last-ditch option to fund your idea is to sell everything you own and put that money towards product development. Selling furniture, clothes, even cars can be an excellent way to finance product development if you don't need those items. Maybe you have a BMW and decide you can live with a used Toyota. If you firmly believe your idea will go on to make *billions*, selling your BMW today should be a no-brainer.

PEOPLE

Make A Deposit

A few years ago I attended a black tie gala held by my local Chamber of Commerce just outside of Atlanta. A Mercedes dealer was being honored for his outstanding contributions to the community and said something during his acceptance speech I'll never forget.

"If you want success in life, make deposits instead of withdrawals."

He went on to explain that most people approach relationships like withdrawing money from a bank. We all know you can't withdraw money from a real bank without first making a deposit, but that's what many people do with relationships. We ask for help without first making ourselves available to help others. When I think of the most successful entrepreneurs I know, they all share a common thread of putting others first. They somehow find time in their busy schedules to add value for others, expecting nothing in return.

When we're in desperate need of help - particularly in the idea stage - it can be quite tempting to seek and take out withdrawals from our relationships. In truth, this is the most critical time to make deposits. Do everything in your power to help others and expect nothing in return. Just as you remember the people who look out for you, others will remember your efforts to make deposits in their lives.

As we move from idea to startup, making deposits becomes more important than ever. New startups have customers to take care of, and no one is more important than your first customers. When I first started Tenrocket, I was blown away by the prevalence of bad business in the world. As it turns out, many businesses - even seemingly successful ones - don't do what they promise their clients. We made a promise to ourselves from day one to never become that kind of company. We designed and implemented checks and balances to penalize ourselves if we failed to meet expectations. People ask me all the time, "How can you afford to offer a 110% money-back guarantee on your projects?". The answer, of course, is that we deserve to lose money if we don't meet our clients expectations. That guarantee forces us to build processes and systems that make it almost impossible for us to fail, and in return, creates a fantastic quality assurance process for our clients. Of course, it's easy to get comfortable with delivering your product as expected, but making deposits is about going beyond expectations. One of the most exciting and enjoyable things you can do as a new startup is build the world's most amazing experience for your clients. We're constantly refining this process at Tenrocket, and this year we'll be doing things like sending surprise gifts to our clients mid-project. Sure it's good business, but it's also a lot of fun.

Eventually, you'll get to the point where you're hiring and managing employees at your startup. These people will quickly become the lifeblood of your company, and it's critically important that you make deposits in their lives. Good leaders understand that happy employees make for successful companies, and do everything they can to empower and promote their staff. Early on at Tenrocket, my business partner Justin and I would celebrate big wins by heading to our favorite coffee shop or grabbing a beer. We'd give each other epic high-fives and tell each other frequently how great a job the other is doing. In the end, these quirks make for the inner fabric of your company culture. It becomes a genuine reflection of who you are as a person, and if you make a point of standing for the empowerment of others, your culture and employees will reflect that same sentiment.

Closing Thoughts

Starting a company is still viewed as one of the most time-consuming, risky, and expensive endeavors in the world. Would-be entrepreneurs face huge barriers to making their ideas a reality, and it's become a right of passage in the startup community to overcome these obstacles and find success on the other side. It seems that the more successful we become as entrepreneurs, the more we forget about our humble beginning as the little guy with a big idea. The most successful entrepreneurs become millionaires and even billionaires, and that makes it difficult to promote and lift up ideas that aren't earth-shattering revelations.

In writing this book, I thought of all the entrepreneurs sitting impatiently at their office desk while brainstorming big ideas for the future. I thought of the college student meticulously studying for final exams, just itching to get out in the real world and prove herself. Most of all, I remembered my own experience of having gigantic barriers standing in the way of what felt like my destiny as a human being.

Starting a company should not have to cost as much as a new Mercedes. It should not require risking the livelihood of entire families, nor should it be an exclusive club reserved only for those willing to jump through enormous hoops to get there. Yes, society needs to take bold leaps forward, but that will only happen when individuals do the same. For the office manager sitting quietly in his cubicle, a bold leap forward might be starting that productivity app he's always envisioned. For the college student, it might mean starting a service company to learn the ins and outs of running a successful business.

We are all pursuing art in some capacity, and art is not born overnight. We forge it in the blood and sweat of the tireless pursuit of our passions. As entrepreneurs, we see art in the exploration of ideas. They are our clay, and we handle them to the best of our ability as we learn how to sculpt. When the world tells us to be more like Michelangelo, here's to choosing instead to be ourselves, understanding that even Michelangelo did not become Michelangelo overnight. Some day people will look to us as examples of the promise of entrepreneurship, and we'll tell them to be exactly who they are.

ABOUT THE AUTHOR

Chris Turner loves new ideas and the people driven to make them real. He has a passion for entrepreneurship and loves growing new companies.

As the co-founder of Tenrocket, he works every day to help people move from "I have an idea" to "I run a company called…". When he's not at Switchyards or a random startup event, you'll find him hanging out with his wife Hannah and son Logan.

SOURCES

http://www.forbes.com/sites/neilpatel/2015/01/16/90-of-startups-will-fail-heres-what-you-need-to-know-about-the-10/

http://www.inc.com/leigh-buchanan/us-entrepreneurship-reaches-record-highs.html

https://www.cbinsights.com/research-unicorn-companies

http://www.statista.com/statistics/326315/global-ice-cream-market-size/

http://www.businessinsider.com/successful-people-who-failed-at-first-2015-7

http://www.telegraph.co.uk/culture/books/10178960/The-Cuckoos-Calling-publishers-embarrassment-at-turning-down-JK-Rowling-detective-novel.html

http://sjinsights.net/2014/09/29/new-research-sheds-light-on-daily-ad-exposures/

https://www.brewersassociation.org/statistics/national-beer-sales-production-data/

http://www.millennialmarketing.com/2014/01/the-millennial-consumer-craves-craft-beer/

www.ingramcontent.com/pod-product-compliance
Lightning Source LLC
Chambersburg PA
CBHW020709180526
45163CB00008B/3014